Thomas Jefferson Miles

To all whom it may concern : the conspiracy of leading men

of the Republican Party to destroy the American Union

proved by their words and acts antecedent and subsequent

to the rebellion

Thomas Jefferson Miles

**To all whom it may concern : the conspiracy of leading men of the Republican
Party to destroy the American Union proved by their words and acts antecedent
and subsequent to the rebellion**

ISBN/EAN: 9783337208066

Printed in Europe, USA, Canada, Australia, Japan

Cover: Foto ©Suzi / pixelio.de

More available books at **www.hansebooks.com**

"TO ALL WHOM IT MAY CONCERN."

THE CONSPIRACY

OF LEADING MEN OF THE REPUBLICAN PARTY

TO DESTROY

THE AMERICAN UNION

PROVED

BY THEIR WORDS AND ACTS

ANTECEDENT AND SUBSEQUENT TO THE REBELLION.

BY

THOMAS JEFFERSON MILES,

OF PHILADELPHIA.

NEW YORK:

PUBLISHED BY J. WALTER & CO.,

19 CITY HALL SQUARE.

1864.

NOT ' BY TH : Pl BLISHERS.

~ EVENTS of the past few years have demonstrated the existence of an organized effort to make important changes in the Government of the United States; not in the legitimate manner provided by the Constitution, but insidiously, stealthily at first, growing bolder by degrees, and at length when circumstances seemed to warrant immunity from personal danger, unblushingly avowed, by the less cautious aiders and abettors of the treasonable.work.

In the accompanying pages, the author, in a clear, logical, and eloquent manner, has grouped numerous startling proofs, and from these argued the case with unusual ability and fairness, and shown that the charge of "conspiracy" is justly applied. But while clear proof is given of a cherished purpose, long entertained, to subvert the Constitution by perverting and destroying its plainest provisions, it does not appear that the design has ever been openly announced with a view of bringing it distinctly and boldly to the notice of the public. On the contrary, when charged with aiming at the subversion of the Government, the answer has been that their purpose was not to destroy, but to save it.

Meantime, a large portion of the people, not understanding the questions at issue, have been unable to discriminate between the real friends of liberty and law, and the secret enemies of both. The crime planned and attempted, has been greater in magnitude and in its contemplated result, than they were prepared to believe possible. Hence, when the charge has been made and repeated, many have regarded it as one of those extravagant accusations which frequently arise from partisan asperity. But the people are becoming hourly more enlightened upon those subjects which enable them to appreciate the contemplated wrong, and they have resolved to know the whole truth of the matter. A severe inquisition will probe this question to the heart. The real conspirators will be known, and will receive the merited rewards of their deeds.

Most respectfully, but earnestly, we urge upon every champion of the Constitution, every friend of civil liberty, to lend his indivdiual influence zealously in the circulation of this most valuable document. Nothing to be compared with it for *immediate* and *important* effect has yet appeared. ONE HUNDRED THOUSAND copies, at least, should be in the hands of the people before the 8th of November. Contributions to this object may be sent to the publishers, and all funds furnished for this purpose, will be immediately used in the gratuitous distribution of the pamphlet.   J. W. & CO.

NEW YORK, *October,* 10, 1864.

"TO ALL WHOM IT MAY CONCERN."

At no other period‧ since the morning of liberty dawned upon this favored land, has it been so manifestly the duty of the people to discard partisan bias, and all those potent influences which distract and mislead the judgment; in order that calmness, soberness, solemnity, and earnestness, may characterize reflection, discussion, and action ; for by these influences alone can our country be saved from *certain, speedy, and irretrievable ruin.* In the halcyon days of the Republic, those good old days of " Virtue, Liberty, and Independence," the political questions which engaged the attention of the people were multifarious. Questions of revenue, of finance, the improvement of harbors and rivers ; the distribution of the proceeds of public lands among the States, and the occupation of those lands by the sturdy pioneer.

My fellow-countrymen, these questions, and many others of like import, were once regarded as possessing vital interest for the people of our common country. Alas! They no longer possess an interest for you.

As when a great calamity casts its gloomy shadow over our individual household, all minor evils are forgotten in the anxiety occasioned by the one overwhelming affliction, so this unspeakable calamity which has visited our national household has driven from our minds all thought of those legitimate governmental questions, whose very discussion was the best indication of peace, contentment, happiness, and prosperity, such as no other people under the broad canopy of heaven were ever permitted to enjoy. No, my countrymen—no! one question alone is worthy of your deliberation now. It is a question that freemen are asking one of another with kindling eye and throbbing heart, WHAT CAN BE DONE TO RESCUE FROM THE GRASP OF DESPOTIC POWER THE PRICELESS JEWEL OF CONSTITUTIONAL LIBERTY ? This is the vital question, that towers in colossal proportions above all others. You, citizens of America, upon the solemn responsibility which you owe, not alone to yourselves, but to latest posterity, must answer on the eighth of November next. Let me adjure you to remember that upon the response which you shall make, is involved all that can make life desirable to an American citizen.

Let us, then, Freemen of America, *resolve* by all the inspiring memories of the past, by all the imperilled interests of the present, by all our anxious hopes in the future, that the Constitution, the laws, and the Union of these States shall be maintained and defended against treason, in every form, whether it be arrayed under the flaunting banner of Southern secession, or under the atrocious and contemptible, because insidious and cowardly black flag of Northern Abolitionism.

Is it not amazing that so many of the honest yeomanry of the country can be so blinded by party prejudice, so trammelled by party discipline as still to array themselves under a banner that for thirty years has had emblazoned upon its folds, in characters so plain that none need misunderstand, those very doctrines of disunion and discord, which are now so falsely charged upon the Democracy of the country? Yet, so it is,—a lamentable fact. Although the rank and file of all political organizations are honest and well meaning, they are liable to be cajoled and misled by wily, selfish, and unscrupulous demagogues, made willing victims of their own destruction.

While history records some examples of voluntary surrender of liberty by the people, under the baleful teachings of artful, ambitious men, its pages will be searched in vain for a parallel to that self-stultification, moral blindness, prejudice, fanaticism, or by whatsoever name it may be called, through whose maddening influence a large portion of the free citizens of this enlightened and most favored land, are, at this very moment, deliberately riveting the manacles of despotism upon their own free limbs.

I most respectfully entreat every fair-minded and reasonable Republican to suspend for a brief season those partisan prejudices which blindfold him to the light of reason, and render him deaf to the voice of fair discussion. I care not to appeal to the passions of men. I prefer to address myself to their honest, sober reflections. Unless, indeed, it may be said,

"O judgment, thou art fled to brutish beasts,
And men have lost their reason!"

Words of wisdom seem to be lost amid the shrieking whirlwind of passion, the tread of marshalled hosts, the clash of glittering steel, the discordant bellowing of ponderous artillery, and the crackling embers of conflagrated cities; and when at length "some dreary pause between," and sympathizing Night has cast her dusky mantle over the horror of these scenes, hark! another sound, more terrible than the din of battle, breaks upon the stillness of the midnight hour. Alas! for that wail of anguish whose woful cadence, rising from fields of carnage, is floated to every cottage and mountain-home throughout the broad area of this once bright and peerless, now bleeding and distracted land.

Let us then, in the first place, endeavor to brush away the cobwebs which the spider, Abolition, has woven about the eyelids of so many conservative and well-meaning men, in order that they may be enlightened in regard to some, at least, of the numerous heresies of the Republican creed: prominent among which, and perhaps the most mischievous, is that of confounding the Administration of the Government with the Government itself. This is a cardinal error, and betrays a misapprehension of the true theory of our governmental structure. A little reflection, unbiased by party zeal, would reveal the nakedness of this fallacy.

Republicans clamor for an unconditional support of the Government, meaning the *Administration*. Democrats contend for an *unconditional* support of the Government, meaning the *Constitution and the laws*.

Republicans argue that the Administration, for the time being, is the Government. Democrats deny the correctness of this proposition.

I hold as an axiom, that the Constitution of the United States, embodying in its provisions the WILL OF THE SOVEREIGN PEOPLE is, *per se*, the *Government* of the United States. That Constitution provides for its own administration in the election by the people of agents, with power to those agents to appoint subordinates. The official titles of said principal agents, their terms of office, their duties and their salaries, being fixed and designated *by the people* in their Constitution. And whenever, and by whomsoever, addition to or subtraction from that fundamental law is attempted, in ever so minute a degree—save in the manner written and provided therein ; or whenever or by whomsoever another law is attempted to be substituted for this supreme law, the person or persons so offending are guilty of, at least, moral treason to the Government of the United States.

How natural that the author of the "Higher Law" doctrine, should also be the author of the following words, addressed to Lord Lyons in November, 1861 :

"My Lord, I can touch a bell on my right hand, and order the arrest of a citizen of Ohio ; I can touch the bell again, and order the imprisonment of a citizen of New York ; and no power on earth, except that of the President, can release them. Can the Queen of England do so much ?"

I wonder if it did not occur to Lord Lyons, when these precious words were uttered, that it might have been better for those "*citizens of Ohio and New York,*" had their forefathers been content to remain subjects of King George the Third. The Queen of England certainly cannot "do so much." There are but few Despots in the world who would *dare* "do so much." Perhaps the Empires of Japan and China, the dominions of the Sultan of Turkey, the King of Dahomey, and the *United States of America!* are the only Governments within whose realms there *can* be done "so much." What higher claim has any Despot ever advanced than the unconditional support of his subjects? The difference between a Despotism and a Republic is in this : that while a Despot claims unconditional obedience from the people to his will ; in a Republic like ours, the sovereign people *demand* unconditional obedience from their agent to their (the people's) will, as expressed in their written Constitution.

To admit that unconditional allegiance is due from the people to the Administration, of their own creation, is to admit that the people resign their sovereignty to the Administration ; and inasmuch as there has been no interregnum between the expiration of one Administration and the commencement of another, it follows, as a logical deduction (according to the theory of the Republicans) that ever since the election of General Washington, we have been merely the *subjects* of a long line of sovereign Administrations! Our familiar vaunt, "the sovereign people," has been a shallow pretence—a delusion.

If the Republican theory be correct, then I admit I have no right, save by permission of my sovereign, to write this address, or, persisting in so doing, I shall have no right to complain if the iron gripe which Despots usually fasten on the throats of those who defy their authority, should clutch at mine.

This is certainly an important consideration, and worthy of the most serious reflection of every citizen, whether Republican or Democrat, who heretofore has indulged the belief that he was one of the SOVEREIGN PEOPLE. Meanwhile, let us turn over a few pages of familiar history. Seventy-seven years ago, on the 17th of September, that matchless work of wisdom, the Federal Constitution, perfect in all its proportions, came forth from the hands of its creators. Go with me, in memory, to the city of Philadelphia, on the 14th of May, 1787. On that day, there assembled in the now venerable Hall of Independence, a Convention, composed of men whose names are written in characters of flame on the scroll of immortality; whose glorious deeds deserve to be recorded on the tablet of every freeman's heart. From the 14th of May to the 17th of September, those sages were engaged in earnest, prayerful deliberation; and what was the burden of their anxiety during all those months?

You, my countrymen, each individual of you—your happiness and mine—your liberties and mine! The great problem to be solved was the construction of a confederative system of Government, while yet preserving, in perfect distinctness and vigor, the sovereignty of each individual State; in order thereby to perpetuate to their latest posterity those inestimable political blessings, which, after seven long years of toil, of blood, of poverty, destitution, and horror, they had wrung from the tyrant of Britain. This was the grand problem, which, during that period, from May until September, claimed the God-like intellect, wisdom, and devotion of men clothed in the vesture of nature's nobility—heroes, patriots, sires—our fathers,—a race of men whom God will vouchsafe to the world but once.

Read the immortal record—James Madison and John Blair of Virginia, the two Pinckneys of South Carolina, Langdon of New Hampshire, Sherman of Connecticut, Alexander Hamilton of New York, Livingston of New Jersey, Franklin, Mifflin, Ingersoll, the two Morris's, and Clymer of Pennsylvania, Dickenson of Delaware, Carroll of Maryland, Williamson of North Carolina, Baldwin of Georgia,—these are some of the names. And then we read the name of one, presiding over that august Convention, who, even amidst such noble band, stands majestically prominent. The peerless example for the study of mankind, created, as it were, to animate our race in every age and in every clime, to ennobling aspirations, and virtuous deeds—a name encircled with the effulgent light of its own undying glory—a name enshrined in the inmost chambers of every heart, where virtue and the love of liberty delight to dwell—the name of one, whom monsters, like Wendell Phillips, Garrison, Cheever, and Beecher desecrate, on the same principle which causes vice and uncleanness to abhor the presence of virtue and purity—the name of one, whose sacred ashes reposing in the bosom of his own beloved Virginia, belong equally to Pennsylvania, New Jersey, New York, and every other State, and will not be surrendered by a patriotic and sturdy yeomanry.

Yes, my fellow-countrymen, at the portals of the tomb of Washington sits the genius of Liberty, State Sovereignty, and Union; and while the echo of fratricidal artillery disturbs the silence of that hallowed spot, let us invoke the lofty spirit of the Father of his country, to exorcise the demon of discord from the land he loved so well; that hate, and passion, and wild fury, and fanaticism may flee the American heart, while love, and reason, and generous counsel, may animate to the great work of rescuing from everlasting ruin, the priceless legacy which he bequeathed to us.

In transmitting to Congress a copy of the Constitution, and the resolutions of the Convention, recommending its submission to the States for ratification, George Washington, who performed that duty, thus wrote :

"The Constitution which we now present, is the result of a spirit of amity, and of that mutual deference and concession, which, the peculiarity of our political situation rendered indispensable. That it is liable to as few exceptions as could reasonably be expected, we hope and believe; that it may promote the lasting welfare of that country so dear to us all, and secure her freedom and happiness is our most ardent wish,"

In his immortal Farewell Address, he writes : "Hence, likewise, they will avoid the necessity of *those overgrown military establishments,* which, *under any form of government, are inauspicious to liberty,* and which are to be regarded as *particularly hostile to republican liberty.*"

Again he writes in the same Address: "The *bases* of our political *systems,* is the right of the people to make and alter their *constitutions* of government; but the Constitution, which at any time exists, *till changed,* by an *explicit* and *authentic* act of the WHOLE PEOPLE, is *sacredly obligatory upon all.* The very idea of the power and the right of the people to *establish* government, presupposes the *duty of every individual* to obey the *established government.*"

Mark the language that Washington uses. It has been said that "*words are things;*" General Washington does not use the singular noun *base* of our political *system,* but he employs the *plural* nouns *bases, systems,* and *constitutions* of Government. I repeat the sentence: "The *bases of our political systems,* is the right of the people to make and alter their *constitutions* of government," &c.

Now, if Washington had written ten folio volumes, upon whose every page he had declared that the Federal government was the creature of the so ereign States, and not that the States are creatures of the Federal government (which is the theory of the present Republican party), he could not have more clearly and emphatically announced his opinion.

Let it be observed, also, that he uses the words "constitution" and "government" synonymously, proving that he regarded the Constitution as the Government. Again he writes:

"The alternate domination of one faction over another, sharpened by the spirit of revenge, natural to party dissension, which, in different ages and countries, has perpetrated the most horrid enormities, is itself a frightful despotism. But this leads at length to a more *formal* and *permanent* despotism. The disorders and miseries which result, gradually incline the minds of men to seek security and repose in the absolute power of an individual; and sooner or later the chief of some prevailing faction, more able or more fortunate than his competitors, turns this disposition to the purposes of his own elevation on the RUINS OF PUBLIC LIBERTY."

"It is important, likewise, that the habits of thinking, in a free country, should inspire caution in those intrusted with its administration, to confine themselves within their *respective constitutional spheres;* avoiding, in the exercise of the powers of one department, to encroach upon another. The spirit of encroachment tends to consolidate the powers of all the departments in one, and thus to create,—whatever the form of government,—a real despotism. A just estimate of that love of power, and proneness to abuse it, which predominates in the human heart, is sufficient to satisfy us of the truth of this position." "If in the opinion of the people, the distribution or modification of the powers be in any particular wrong, let it be corrected by an amendment, in the way which the Constitution designates. BUT LET THERE BE NO CHANGE BY USURPATION, for though this, in one instance, may be the instrument of good, it is the customary weapon, by which *free governments are destroyed.* The precedent must always greatly overbalance, in permanent evil, any partial or transient benefit which the use can, at any time, yield."

In these extracts, you have Washington's opinion of the Constitution. Says James Madison, in his first inaugural address, delivered in 1809:

"Prefer in *all cases, amicable discussion, and reasonable accommodations of differences, to a decision of them by an appeal to arms;* to hold the Union of the States as the basis of their peace and happiness; to support the Constitution, which is the cement of the Union, *as well in its limitations as in its authorities;* to respect the rights and authorities *reserved to the States, and to the people,* as equally incorporated with, and *essential* to the success of the general system;" "to preserve in their full energy, the other salutary provisions, in behalf of *private* and *personal* rights, and of the *freedom of the press.*" "Always remembering that an armed and trained MILITIA is the firmest bulwark of republics—that without standing *armies, their liberty can never be in danger,* NOR WITH LARGE ONES SAFE!"

Said Thomas Jefferson, in his first inaugural, in 1801:

"All, too, will bear in mind this sacred principle, that though the will of the majority is, in all cases, to prevail, that will, to be *rightful,* must be *reasonable;* that the minority possess their *equal* rights, which equal laws *must protect,* and to *violate,* would be *oppression.*" "And let us reflect, that, having banished from our land that religious intolerance under which mankind so long bled and suffered, we have yet gained little, if we countenance a *political* intolerance as despotic, as wicked, and capable of as bitter and bloody persecutions."

Again, Mr. Jefferson writes:

"The support of the State governments in all their rights, as the *most competent* administrations for our domestic concerns, and the surest bulwarks against anti-republican tendencies;" "A JEALOUS CARE OF THE RIGHT OF ELECTION BY THE PEOPLE. The supremacy of the civil over the military authority, economy in the public expense, that labor may be lightly burdened. Freedom of religion, freedom of the press, and freedom of person, under the protection of the *habeas corpus,* and trials by juries impartially selected. These principles form the bright constellation which has gone before us, and guided our steps through an age of revolution and reformation. The wisdom of our sages, and blood of our heroes, have been devoted to their attainment; they should be the creed of our political faith, the text of civic instruction, the touchstone, by which to try the services of *those we trust*; and should we wander from them in moments of error or alarm, let us hasten to retrace our steps, and to regain the road which alone leads to peace, liberty, and safety."

Says Chief-Justice Story, a name universally esteemed, referring to the high responsibilities of the people, to preserve their Constitution from usurping power:

"*It must perish*, if there be not that vital spirit in the people, which alone can nourish, sustain, and direct all its movements. It is in vain that Statesmen shall form plans of government, in which the beauty and harmony of a republic shall be embodied in visible order, shall be built up on solid substructions, and adorned by every useful ornament, if the inhabitants suffer the silent power of time to dilapidate its walls, or crumble its massy supporters into dust; if the assaults from without are never *resisted*, and the rottenness and mining from within are never guarded against, who can preserve the rights and liberties of the people, when they shall be *abandoned by themselves?* Who shall keep watch in the Temple, when the watchmen sleep at their posts? Who shall call on the people to redeem their possessions, and revive the republic, when their hands have deliberately and corruptly surrendered them to the oppressor, and have built the prisons, or dug the graves of their own friends? This dark picture, it is to be hoped, will never be applicable to the Republic of America; and yet it affords a warning, which, like all the lessons of past experience, we are not permitted to disregard; America, free, happy, and enlightened as she is, must rest the preservation of her rights and liberties upon the virtue, independence, justice, and sagacity of the people. *If either fail, the* REPUBLIC IS GONE. Its shadow may remain with all the pomp, and circumstance, and trickery of government, but its vital power will have departed. In America, the demagogue may rise as well as elsewhere. He is the natural, though spurious growth of Republics; and, like the courtier, he may, by his blandishments, delude the ears and blind the eyes of the people, to their own destruction. If ever the day shall arrive, in which the best talents and the best virtues shall be driven from office by intrigue or corruption, by the ostracism of the press, or the still more unrelenting persecution of party legislation, THE GOVERNMENT will cease to be national. It will be wise by accident, and bad by sytem."

Montesquieu declares that

"The political liberty of the citizen is a tranquillity of mind, arising from the opinion *each person has of his safety*. The enjoyment of liberty, and even its support and preservation, consists in every man being allowed to *speak his thoughts and lay open his sentiments*."

In a letter from that great statesman, Silas Wright, dated April 9, 1847, he writes:

"No one familiar with the affairs of our Government can have failed to notice how large a proportion of our statesmen appear never to have read the Constitution of the United States, with a careful reference to its *precise language and exact provisions*, but rather, as occasion presents, seem to exercise their ingenuity, unfortunately too often powerful and powerfully exerted to stretch both to the line of what they at the moment consider EXPEDIENT."

Said that enlightened statesman and scholar, John McPherson Berrien, of Georgia:

"A knowledge of the Constitution, whichis for the most part plain and simple in its provisions, would often enable the citizen to spurn indignantly the efforts of demagogues to mislead him, and awaken him to a deeper sense of gratitude for the privileges which he is permitted to enjoy."

On the 13th of February, 1847, George M. Dallas wrote these words:

"It [the Constitution] should form the rudimental basis of American thought, by being made a perpetually recurring object of memory."

I will conclude these quotations with one from the great expounder himself, though they might be continued almost indefinitely : on the 11th of December, 1850, Daniel Webster, then near the close of his useful life, thus wrote:

"The Constitution of the United States is a written instrument, a recorded *fundamental law* ; it is the bond and the *only* bond of the Union of these States ; it is all that gives us a national character. Almost every man in the country is capable of reading it, and that which so deeply concerns all, should be made easily accessible to all."

These are some of the recorded opinions of sages, statesmen, and philosophers, in relation to the Constitution of the United States—most of them Democrats. Now, let us look at the published opinions of the leaders of the abolitionized Republican party. Contrast is at least an artistic arrangement.

Bear in mind, if you please, that the Constitution must be accepted or rejected as a whole. It was so adopted, and not one line or syllable can be rejected without endangering the whole system of government, of which it is the life.

The fourth article just as clearly recognizes the right to hold property in slaves as the fifth article recognizes the right to alter and amend the instrument itself. One article is just as obligatory upon the people as another, and any person or persons who would endeavor to escape that obligation by setting up "a higher law," a law of sentiment to be obeyed in preference to the Constitution, whenever its provisions conflict with their tender consciences, prove themselves *traitors* to the Government of the United States. And this is the kind of treason that has produced this civil war, and deluged the land in fratricidal blood.

I now deliberately charge the leaders of the so-called Republican, but really Abolition party, with a premeditated conspiracy to destroy the Constitution of the United States, and per consequence, the American Union. Mark, I say, *leaders* of this party, for, as I have already remarked, the rank and file of one party are just as honest as those of the other, but deceived and betrayed.

Now, to the proof of this serious charge. In cases of capital crime circumstantial evidence, where the chain is unbroken, has been regarded by writers on criminal law as the safest kind of proof upon which to find a righteous verdict. We have both circumstantial and positive evidence upon which to rest our case.

The nomination of Abraham Lincoln, at Chicago, was only one scene in one act of this wicked and bloody drama. Many scenes have been enacted since, but like the play within the play, in the third act of Hamlet, there will, I apprehend, arise such an infernal commotion among the audience that the conspirators will be driven in discomfiture from the stage, appalled at the picture of their own diabolical murder. Said one of the high priests of their party, one who has received distinguished courtesies at the hands of the President while in Washington, and who was invited by a majority of the Senate to a seat on the floor of the Senate Chamber; an honor rarely accorded, and only to those who have distinguished themselves in the service of their country, and to foreign Ambassadors—said Wendell Phillips :

" The Constitution of our fathers was a mistake. *Tear it to pieces, and make a better one.* Don't say the machine is out of order; it is in order; it does what its framers intended—protect slavery. Our claim is *Disunion, breaking up of the States!* I have shown you that our work cannot be done under our institutions."

"*This Union is a lie! The American Union is an imposture, a covenant with death, and an agreement with hell.* * * * *I am for its overthrow.*"

Said Lloyd Garrison :

" Up with the flag of DISUNION, that we may have a free and glorious Republic of our own ; and when the hour shall come, the hour will have arrived that shall witness the overthrow of slavery."

Here is what Phillips said of the Republican party, when it was organized as a sectional party, and it will be noticed how well and how truly he pictured it :

" No man has a right to be surprised at this state of things. It is just what we [Abolitionists and Disunionists] have attempted to bring about. It is the first sectional party ever organized in this country. It does not know its own face, and calls itself national—it is *sectional.* The Republican party is a party of the North, *pledged against the South.*"

Garrison, in his *Liberator,* said still more explicitly :

" The Republican party is moulding public sentiment in the right direction for the specific work the Abolitionists are striving to accomplish, viz. : *The dissolution of the Union, and the abolition of Slavery throughout the land.*"

All the while that the Abolitionists were talking thus boldly, the Republican leaders pretended to the people that Garrison and Phillips did not represent their sentiments ; but let it be remembered that *they* expressed most substantially the same sentiments, yet in more vague and uncertain language. Said Abraham Lincoln in his famous controversy with Judge Douglas :

" *I believe this Government cannot endure permanently half slave and half free.*"

That is, that it cannot endure as Washington formed it, and as it existed for seventy years. Mr. Garrison was of exactly the same opinion ; and, though Mr. Lincoln does not say all that Mr. Garrison does, yet the person must be stupid who cannot see what Mr. Lincoln's real meaning is. And if any proof were needed of the identity of their principles, it is to be found in the fact that Mr. Lincoln has at last openly come to Garrison's platform.

William H. Seward, in his celebrated Ohio speech, said :

"It [slavery] can and must be abolished, and you and I must do it. * * Correct your own error, *that slavery has Constitutional guarantees* which may not be released, and ought not to be relinquished. * * * You will soon bring the parties of the country into an effective aggression upon slavery."

Mark the words, "*aggression upon slavery!*" and also the denial of the plain Constitutional provision guaranteeing the right to hold slaves. N. P. Banks, now one of Mr. Lincoln's Major-Generals, said in a speech delivered in Maine, in 1855, and while Governor of Massachusetts:

"Although I am not one of that class of men who cry for the preservation of the Union; *though I am willing, in a certain state of circumstances,* TO LET IT SLIDE, I have no fear for its perpetuation. But, let me say, if the chief object of the people of this country be to maintain and propagate chattel property in man—in other words, human slavery—THIS UNION CANNOT AND OUGHT NOT TO STAND."

Now, I would ask, in all candor, suppose a prominent Democrat had uttered those sentiments, would he not have been scouted by his party as one infected with political leprosy? Did the Republican party so treat Governor Banks? No, indeed; but the very next session of Congress—the session of 1856—they elected him Speaker of the national House of Representatives!

Still later—in 1858—in a speech in Massachusetts, we find Mr. Banks turning prophet, and predicting a "*military dictatorial Government*" in this country. He had no faith in the stability of "*free institutions.*" He said :

"I can conceive of a time when this Constitution shall not be in existence ; *when we shall have an absolute military dictatorial Government,* transmitted from age to age, with men at its head who are made rulers by military commission, or who claim an hereditary right to govern those over whom they are placed."

Senator Wade, of Ohio, at a mass meeting in Maine, the same at which Mr. Banks spoke, gave utterance to the following treasonable sentiments :

"The only salvation of the Union, is to be found in divesting it of all taint of human slavery. *Or, let us sweep away this remnant which we call a Union.* I go for a Union where all men are equal, or for NO UNION at all ; and I go for right."

And, as if to mark their approval of such doctrines, the Republicans of Ohio, the very next year, re-elected this disunionist to the Senate of the United States. His brother, Hon. Edwin Wade, has, for a number of years, occupied a seat in the House of Representatives, and we find him, in a speech delivered in the House, August 2, 1856, indorsing the treasonable doctrine of his Senatorial brother. We quote :

"Sir, if the Constitution and the Union are to be used as instruments for propagating human bondage, they cannot be preserved—*neither is it desirable that they should.* The spirit which has taken possession of the slaveholders and their base tools, the Democracy of the free States, is the unclean thing of slavery propagandism; and just as sure as animal life perishes in mephitic gases, so sure is it that the Constitution and Union must perish when smothered in the fond embraces of these allies of human slavery."

"Allies of human slavery!"—Washington, Jefferson, Madison, Jackson, Polk, &c.

The Hon. Sidney Dean, of Connecticut, is in favor of dissolving the Union, unless freedom—that is, the freedom of the black race—shall be inaugurated in this country. We quote from a speech of his delivered in the House of Representatives, July 23, 1856 :

"The issue of all, the reason of all, the basis of all this lies in the simple question, shall freedom or slavery be the ruling, predominant feature of the model Republic of the world ? That question can be answered in one way. Freedom, human, personal freedom, the fulfilment of the great sentiment, 'that all men are created free and equal.'"

Mark the lying interpolation. The words of the Declaration of Independence are, "all men are created equal." The word *free* does not occur, and yet it is constantly quoted by abolition speakers and writers, as the *Honorable* Mr. Dean has quoted it. This is one of the methods by which the people are cheated. He proceeds,

"This will be the national ruling of this country for future centuries, or the sun of its past glory will set in drapery crimsoned in its own blood ere it reaches a century of its existence."

Judge Rufus P. Spaulding, a delegate to the Republican Convention, in 1856, and also to the Convention that nominated Mr. Lincoln, said in a speech made in the former Convention :

"In case of the alternatives being presented, of the continuance of slavery or a dissolution of the Union, I AM FOR DISSOLUTION, AND I CARE NOT HOW QUICK IT COMES."

There is no begging the question with Judge Spaulding; he speaks the sentiments of his party in plain Saxon.

Said the Hon. Horace Mann, of Massachusetts, in a speech delivered on the floor of the national House of Representatives:

"I have only to add, under a full sense of my responsibility to my country and my God, I deliberately say, BETTER DISUNION, BETTER A SERVILE WAR, better any thing that God in His providence shall send, than an extension of the bonds of slavery."

Charles Sumner, the Chairman of the Committee on Foreign Relations in the United States Senate, while advocating the abolition of slavery in a speech delivered in Faneuil Hall, Boston, November 2d, 1855, said :

"God forbid, *that for the sake of the Union*, we should sacrifice the very thing for which the Union was made."

Still later, on the 19th and 20th of May, 1855, in a speech delivered in the Senate, Mr. Sumner held this revolutionary language :

"Already has the muster begun. The strife is no longer local, but national. Even now while I speak portents hang on all the arches of the horizon, threatening to darken the broad land, *which already yawns with· the mutterings of* CIVIL WAR."

Mr. Sumner, perfectly understanding the dark secrets of his party, heard, even in 1855. "the mutterings of our present deplorable civil war!" William II. Seward, in his speech in the Senate, April 9, 1856, said:

"He who found a river in his path, and sat down to wait for the flood to pass away, was not more unwise than he who expects the agitation of slavery to cease while the love of freedom animates the bosoms of mankind."

And then, after showing that this agitation will lead to war between the North and the South, Mr. Seward suggests to the Pacific States that then would be their time to withdraw from the Union. He continues:

"Then the free States and the slave States of the Atlantic, divided and warring with each other, would disgust the free States of the Pacific, and they would have *abundant cause and justification* for WITHDRAWING FROM A UNION productive no longer of peace, safety, and liberty to themselves, and no longer holding up the cherished hopes of mankind."

This is South Carolina doctrine.

Again, in his speech at Albany, October 12, 1855, Mr. Seward said:

"Slavery is not, and never can be, perpetual. It will be overthrown either peacefully and lawfully under this Constitution, or it will work the subversion of the Constitution, together with its own overthrow. Then the SLAVEHOLDERS WOULD PERISH IN THE STRUGGLE."

Again, in his speech in the Senate, March 11, 1850, Mr. Seward threatens the South with "civil war" unless they emancipate their slaves. He says:

"When this answer shall be given it will appear that the question of dissolving the Union is a complex question that embraces the fearful issue whether the Union shall stand and slavery under the steady, peaceful action of moral, social, and political causes, be removed by gradual voluntary effort, and with compensation, *or whether the* UNION SHALL BE DISSOLVED, *civil war ensue, bringing on violent but complete and immediate emancipation.* We are now arrived at that stage when that crisis can be foreseen—when we must foresee it. It is directly before us. Its shadow is upon us."

In plain words, Mr. Seward says to the South: You can have union and the gradual emancipation of slavery, or you *shall* have disunion, civil war, and immediate emancipation! This, in plain English, was his proposition.

The Hon. Francis E. Spinner, Register of the Treasury Department under Mr. Chase, said, in a speech delivered in 1856, alluding to the possible failure of the Republicans in the effort to elect Frémont:

"The free North would be left to the choice of peaceful DISSOLUTION OF THE UNION, A CIVIL WAR, *which would end in the same,* or an unconditional surrender of every principle held dear by freemen."

That most charitable, meek, and liberal-minded apostle of Abolitionism, Henry Ward Beecher, said in 1856, in a speech at New Haven, Ct., where he proclaimed that "a Sharp's rifle was a truly moral agency:"

"If this peaceful remedy [the ballot-box] should fail to be applied this year, then the people will count the cost wisely, and decide for themselves, boldly and firmly, which is the better way, to RISE IN ARMS AND THROW OFF A GOVERNMENT *worse than that of old King George*, or endure it another four years, and then vote again."

In the same speech, Mr. Beecher thus denounced the Constitution of the United States:

"The Constitution is the cause of every division which this vexed question of slavery has ever occasioned in this country. It has been the fountain and father of our troubles, by attempting to hold together, as reconciled, two opposing principles, which will not harmonize nor agree. The only hope of the slave is, *over the ruins of the Government and of the American Church. The dissolution of the Union is the abolition of slavery.*"

James Watson Webb, Mr. Lincoln's minister to Brazil, was a delegate to the Convention that nominated Mr. Lincoln, and also the Convention that nominated Frémont. In his speech, in that Convention, he gave utterance to the following words, which were received with tumultuous cheering and cries of "good:"

"They [the slaveholders] tell you they are willing to abide by the ballot-box, and are willing to make that last appeal. If we fail there, what then? We will drive it back, sword in hand; and, so help me God, believing that to be right, I am with them. [Loud cheers and cries of "Good!"] Northern gentlemen, on your action depends the result. You may, with God's blessing, present to this country a name, rallying around it all the elements of the Opposition, and thus we will become so strong that, through the ballot-box, we will save the country. But if a name be presented on which we may not rally, and the consequence is *civil war*—nothing more, nothing less, but civil war—I ask, then, what is our first duty?"

In the same Convention, the Hon. Erastus Hopkins used these words:

"If peaceful means fail us, and we are driven to the last extremity, when ballots are useless, then we will make bullets effective."

The Hon. John P. Hale, United States Senator from New Hampshire, was also a delegate to the Convention, and addressed it at length. He congratulated the Convention upon the spirit of unanimity with which it had done its work. He said:

"I believe that this is not so much a Convention to change the Administration of the Government, as to say whether there shall be any Government to be administered. You have assembled not to say whether this Union shall be preserved, but to say whether it shall be a blessing or a scorn and hissing among nations."

On the 31st of May, 1848, he said: "Let the consequences be what they may, I am willing to place myself upon the principle of human right; to stand where the word of God and my own conscience concur in placing me, and there bid defiance to all consequences. And in the end, if this Union, bound as it is to associations, has no other principle of cement than the blood of human slavery, *let it sunder.*"

Again, on the 12th of July, he said:

"*All the horrors of dissolution I can look steadfastly in the face*, before I could look to that moral ruin which must fall upon us when we have so far prostituted ourselves as to become the pioneers of slavery in the Territories."

In the Senate on the 26th February, 1856, he said: "I thank God that the indications of the present day seem to promise that the North have at last got to the wall, and will go no farther. I hope so. The Senator says there may be a power that shall say 'Thus far shalt thou go, and no farther.' [Good! good!] Sir, I hope it will come, and if it comes to blood, let blood come. No, sir, if that issue must come, let it come, and it cannot come too soon. Sir, Puritan blood has not always shrunk from even those encounters; and when the war has been proclaimed with the knife, and the knife to the hilt, the steel has sometimes glistened in their hands; and when the battle was over, they were not always second best."

Carl Schurz, appointed by Mr. Lincoln minister to Spain, was a delegate to the Chicago Convention, and took a very active part in securing the nomination of Mr. Lincoln. Hear him, in 1860, in a speech at St. Louis:

"May the God in human nature be aroused and pierce the very soul of our nation with an energy that shall sweep as with the besom of destruction this abomination from the land. You call this revolution. It is. In this we need revolution; *we will have it! Let it come!*"

Horace Greeley, to whom Mr. Lincoln is indebted for his nomination at Chicago, has always boldly advocated disunion:

"If the Cotton States shall become satisfied that they can do better out of the Union than in it, we insist on letting them go in peace. The right to secede may be a revolutionary one, but it exists, nevertheless. * * * We must ever resist the right of any State to remain in the Union and nullify or destroy the laws thereof. To withdraw from the Union is quite another matter. Whenever a considerable section of our Union shall deliberately resolve to go out, we shall resist all coercive measures designed to keep it in. We hope never to live in a republic whereof one section is pinned to another by bayonets."—*Tribune* of November 9, 1860.

"If the Cotton States unitedly and earnestly wish to withdraw peacefully from the Union, we think they should be allowed to do so. Any attempt to compel them by force to remain, would be contrary to the principles enunciated in the immortal Declaration of Independence, contrary to the fundamental ideas on which human liberty is based."—*Tribune,* November 26, 1860.

"If it [the Declaration of Independence] justifies the secession from the British empire of three millions of colonists in 1776, we do not see why it would not justify the secession of five millions of Southerners from the Union in 1861."—*Tribune,* December 17, 1860.

"Whenever it shall be clear that the great body of the Southern people have become conclusively alienated from the Union, and anxious to escape from it, we will do our best to forward their views."—*Tribune,* February 23, 1862.

Thaddeus Stevens, the Chairman of the Committee of Ways and Means in the last Congress, and the acknowledged leader of the Republican party, said recently, in a speech at Lancaster:

"If I believed that the object of this war was to restore the Union as it was, including slavery, I would be against the war."

Mr. M. E. Conway, a Republican member of Congress from Kansas, in a fit of disgust at the "fast and loose" game of Gerrit Smith and others, concludes a letter to Mr. Greeley in these words:

"As to the Union, I would not give a cent for it, unless it stood as a guarantee for freedom to every man, woman, and child within its entire jurisdiction. I consider the idea that every thing must be sacrificed to the Union utterly preposterous. What was the Union made for? That we should sacrifice ourselves to it? I, for one, would beg to be excused. As things stand I would sacrifice the Union to Freedom any morning before breakfast."

Ex-Governor Johnston is in favor of "*trampling* upon the Constitution" if it stands in the way of "preserving!"—(Heaven save the mark!) —"the nation!"

These remarks of Governor Johnston were *applauded* at the Chestnut street League in Philadelphia.

The atrocious Alfred N. Gilbert, addressing the Philadelphia Union League, said he "would see every woman and child in the South perish," rather than that the Abolition party should fail in its objects.

Abraham Lincoln, when a member of Congress, in a speech delivered on the floor of the House, January 12th, 1848, boldly and emphatically advocated the doctrine of secession. He said:

"Any people, anywhere, being inclined and having the power have a *right to rise up and shake off the existing government, and form a new one that suits them better*. This is a most valuable, a most sacred right, a right which we hope and believe is to liberate the world. Nor is this right confined to cases in which the *whole* people of an existing government may choose to exercise it. *Any portion* of such people that *can* may revolutionize and make their own of so much of the territory as they inhabit. More than this, a *majority of any portion* of such people may revolutionize, putting down a minority, intermingled with or near about them, who may oppose their movements. It is a quality of revolution not to go by old lines or old laws, but to break up both and to make new ones."

This speech will be found recorded in the Congressional reports of that session.

So much for a portion only of what has been said and written. These quotations might be continued almost without limit. Now, what has been done?

And here it is proper to observe that the Republican party was organized, not as a *national*, but as a *sectional* or geographical party. The first meeting called for the purpose of its organization, was held on the 26th of September, 1854, at Auburn, New York, the home of William H. Seward. The object, as stated, was to "organize a Republican party, which should represent the friends of freedom." On that occasion General Bruce said: "They *would raise a thunder that would shake Southern Slavery to its very centre*." In proof that its organization was purely sectional, the following resolution, offered by General Granger, was adopted:

"Resolved, That we recommend that a Convention of delegates *from the Free States*, equal in number to their representatives in Congress, re-

2

spectively, be held at the city of Syracuse, on the 4th of July, 1856, to nominate candidates for the Presidency and Vice-Presidency of the *United States*, for the next Presidential election."

The resolution was adopted with "tremendous cheering." Dr. Snodgrass moved to call this the *Republican party*. The Convention then adjourned *sine die*. The place of meeting of the proposed Convention was afterwards changed from Syracuse to Philadelphia, where, in pursuance of the foregoing resolution, they met and nominated Frémont.

In 1860, the delegates met at Chicago, and nominated Lincoln. During the proceedings of that Convention, Judge Jessup rose and said :

That he desired to amend a verbal mistake in the name of the party, It was printed in the resolutions "*National* Republican party." He wished to strike out the word *National*, as that was not the name by which the party was *properly* known.

The correction was made. Thus originated the sectional party now in power, against which the NATIONAL Democratic party is contending.

The limits of this address will not suffice to notice one-tenth part of the acts of these conspirators against our national Constitution, which, if all grouped together, would form a picture of political and moral depravity appalling in its hideousness.

I must be content to select some of the more prominent and glaring.

I pass over the infamous "personal liberty laws," adopted by Republican Legislatures, designed to render nugatory the fourth clause of the second section of the fourth article of the Constitution.

I pass by the "Emigrant Aid Societies," the "John Brown raid," and the circulation of the atrocious "Helper book," with its indorsement by sixty-eight Republican Senators and members. And here let it be observed, that it is perfectly consistent with the philosophy of the human mind, that it may be gradually moulded and prepared by plausible arts and skill, playing upon the passions and prejudices, and even upon the purest and noblest impulses of the heart, until a species of moral insanity seizes upon and drags its victim down to irretrievable ruin.

And this is the unfortunate condition to which a large portion of the honest yeomanry of our country have been reduced by the infernal sorcery of the fiends of Abolitionism. With plausible sophistry they have poisoned the delicate, sensitive, and impressionable mind of a large portion of the mothers and daughters, and through their influence, the male youth of our land; holding up to distempered fancy, highly colored pictures of a false philanthropy, until at length the glorious institutions of our Fathers have become subordinate to the dangerous sentimentalism of a "higher law" doctrine, promulgated as a political dogma by him who sits as prime minister at the right hand of Abraham the First. No free people ever lost their liberties by sudden assault.

The citadel of AMERICAN liberty, especially, could not have been stormed without overwhelming discomfiture to the assailants. The attempt has been made to take it by siege, by gradual approaches, by "parallels," to use a now familiar military term. Declarations and proclamations are issued, and acts performed to-day that could not have been declared or performed six months ago. Things were said and done six months ago that could not have been said or done six months previously, and so on to the beginning of the chapter, when Mr. Lincoln delivered his inaugural, declaring that he had "no constitutional right" to molest or interfere with any of the local institutions of the rebellious States, and when, in December, 1861, Mr. Seward addressed his famous circular letter to our ambassadors at the several courts of Europe, explicitly and emphatically declaring the same cardinal truth.

The worst passions of the human heart, disguised under the mantles of charity, philanthropy, and expediency, have been employed with diabolical skill and success, to steal away the precious birthright of American liberty.

If Satan were only permitted to wage his warfare against our fallen race in all the hideousness, wherein he is represented to appear in the regions of Pandemonium, there would be no need of warning the people against him; all men would flee in terror at his approach; but, for some inscrutable purpose, he is permitted to assume many bright and alluring forms. Perhaps there is no garment in all his extensive sulphurous, wardrobe, which he wears with greater success in his infernal mission, than the drab cloak of canting hypocritical philanthropy.

The horrible condition of our country to-day, is the result, or natural sequence, of the Puritanical meddlesomeness and selfishness of the witch-burning semi-infidel portion of the New England population. There are, it is true, some large-hearted, noble people in New England; those who, to-day, stand up in their manhood, vainly, and almost hopelessly, struggling against a flood of fanaticism: men, for instance, like the venerable Bishop Hopkins, of Vermont, and Winthrop, of Massachusetts, especially merit the eulogy and sympathy of every champion of the Constitution.

New England traded in negroes—in the Convention that framed the Constitution, she voted to extend the slave-trade twenty years, viz., until 1808—brought them in ships from their native Africa, worked them on her land, until its impoverished soil rendered it no longer profitable; and then, having made a " smart" bargain (you may rely upon that), sold them to her Southern neighbors, whom she has never ceased to envy, in the wealth which the rich Southern soil has enabled them to derive from this species of labor.

By amazing shrewdness and tact in political manœuvring, New England, by means of her tariff, has always largely profited from the *labor* of the slaves, while free from the expense or trouble of supporting them; but her inordinate avarice and greed of wealth, has always induced a covetous hankering for the possession of that fair domain, whose princely harvests have supplied nearly four-fifths of the vast exportations of our magnificent commerce. And if she could only get possession of those rich cotton and rice plantations of Georgia and South Carolina, having first confiscated the soil and exterminated the owners; and could fill her coffers with pelf, by retaining all the negroes in a condition of bondage, it would be found before a great while, that one-half the population of Massachusetts, Vermont, and the other New England States, would be engaged in raising cotton and rice, by the use of slave labor (the only kind of labor, indeed, by which those staples can profitably be raised). The only difference would be, that for every bale of cotton which the moderately worked negro now produces, his sweat, yea, and blood, too, would be taxed to produce *three.*

Heaven help the poor negro, if he should ever change his present for New England masters! Then would he know the bitterness of slavery! In this connection, it is worthy of remark, that in those States where Abolitionism is most rampant, are found the smallest number of free negroes.

I have shown that the President, when a member of Congress, advocated Secession, or revolutionary doctrine; that all, or most of the leaders of the Republican party, advocated violent revolutionary doctrines; that Mr. Seward, promulgated as a political dogma, that there was a law higher than the Constitution of the United States, to which the fundamental law of the land was declared to be subordinate; that there was an "irrepressible conflict" between the slave labor of the South and the free labor of the North, in the face of the fact, that the country had advanced from infancy to colossal maturity, under these two systems of labor; showing that, so far from there being a conflict, the two systems have worked together in beautiful harmony; the producing slave labor of the South, and the manufacturing and commercial enterprise of the North, operating harmoniously; a system, in which there was no jar, until the discordant element of New England fanaticism, got the machinery into disorder. The Abolition Chicago Convention, was only a new act in the drama. The most radical abolitionists in the Convention—those who had preached the strongest disunion doctrines—were the most urgent advocates of Mr. Lincoln's nomination, over Mr. Seward and all other candidates. Horace Greeley was particularly active in securing his nomination. Seward was not trusted by Greeley, Phillips, Lovejoy, and the radicals of their complexion. They apprehended that after using the "American citizens of African descent," until he (Seward) should be safely seated in the Presidential chair, he would abandon the negro and "Tylerize" their party; hence, they would not trust him. The programme had, doubtless, been arranged: Seward was to be used until the eleventh hour, to preach his "irrepressible" philosophy, and then to be thrown overboard. The man who had declared that "the government could not permanently exist half slave and half free," was to be their standard-bearer, and so Abraham Lincoln was nominated.

I pass over the scenes of the Presidential canvass, the deplorable division and wasting of the strength of the Democratic party; pass over those days, when every Democratic heart was sad at the prospect of triumph, for the first time in our history, of a purely sectional party; well remembering the warning voice of Washington in his Farewell Address, and the warnings of all the great Statesmen, as well in the later, as in the early periods of the Republic, all of whom seemed to believe that this was the only strain which the Union was not strong enough to bear. I pass over those ribald jests and taunts of the Republicans, who, when

Democratic voices were raised in earnest remonstrance, supplication, and warning, against the election of a president committed to a sectional platform, called them in derision, "Union-savers," "Union-shriekers," and other opprobrious epithets, as now the same men call Democrats, "Copperheads," and "traitors," in their spite: because what was then predicted, has been verified by the ghastly logic of events, and because the same warning voice that was disregarded then, is again raised, in pleading accents for the preservation of all that remains of the dearest rights of American freemen.

As the Democracy truly predicted in 1860, so now the same patriotic voice is heard, crying aloud, "to all whom it may concern," proclaiming to their misguided countrymen, that, dreadful as are the present evils, they are small in comparison with the calamities that are in store for the people, if the present Administration, with its ruinous policy of conducting the war for conquest, subjugation, confiscation, and emancipation, instead of for the preservation of the Union under the Constitution of our fathers, shall be continued during the ensuing four years.

Passing all these scenes, I beg leave to remind you of the condition of the country between the period of Mr. Lincoln's election and his inauguration; State after State, deliberately holding conventions and passing ordinances of secession—assigning as a reason therefor, that the incoming Administration was committed to an invasion of their Constitutional rights; the people everywhere throughout the Northern and Border States in a condition of wild excitement and alarm; while there, at Springfield, sat the President elect, one line of assurance from whose pen at that juncture might have been potential in averting the horrors that have ensued; and although he was adjured to write but a single line, and innumerable letters were addressed to him from every quarter, imploring him to speak or write but a word, his ear remained deaf to every appeal. His voice was silent, while the gallant ship, freighted with the dearest earthly hopes of humanity, was struggling in the trough of a tempestuous sea of passion. He who had been clothed with a moral power for good or for evil, such as but few in history have ever possessed, chose the evil, and refused to utter one syllable of assurance, by which the frenzied passions of the hour might have been calmed, and the awful burden of grief and anxiety lifted from the oppressed and bleeding heart of the Nation.

No, fellow-countrymen, this was not in the programme! Will it be said, in explanation of this inexplicable silence, that to have spoken or written would have done no good? I ask, could it by any possibility have done harm? When men are honestly anxious to avert a calamity, do they not speak and act? When your child is sick, does not your anxiety to have his malady cured induce you to act promptly—to try every remedy which is placed within reach? or do you sit down idly, and crack unseemly jokes? He who would thus act, even in the case of an individual, would be justly execrated as a monster of depravity. What then must be thought of one who would so conduct himself when the national life was threatened—his country trembling and writhing in the throes of dissolution!

History records that Nero, the monster of antiquity, fiddled while Rome was *burning.* The President will be fortunate if the impartial pen of history shall fail to record that Lincoln jested while his country was *dying!*

At length the President leaves Springfield, to travel towards the Capital. In his journey thence, did he manifest that gravity of deportment which might reasonably have been expected, under the circumstances, would have marked the conduct of him who had been chosen to occupy the chair of Washington? No; he talked flippantly about an "artificial crisis;" he talked about "his whiskers;" he indulged in humorous jests about "nobody being hurt;" and finally, capped the climax of folly in the memorable night journey from Harrisburg to the national Capital, disguised in the costume of a tartan cap, and enveloped in the ample folds of a long military cloak.

Having reached the Capital in safety, we find, in the character of the inaugural ceremonies, the natural fruit of those revolutionary doctrines which himself and his wily associates had taught for so many years. The cup of American humiliation was filled when a President of the United States was inaugurated under the protection of drawn sabres and glistening bayonets.

"Oh, what a fall was there, my countrymen! Then you and I, and all of us fell down, while bloody treason flourished over us."

And still I might continue, in the language of the immortal bard (only paraphrasing a little) :

"Ah, now you *weep,* and I perceive you *feel* the dint of pity—good friends—kind friends—let me not stir your hearts and minds to any sudden flood of mutiny; they that have done this deed are *honorable.* What *private* griefs they have, alas, I know not, that made them do it! They are wise and honorable, and will, no doubt, with *reason* answer you. I come not, friends, to *steal* away your hearts! I am no *orator,* as *Everett* is. But as you know me all, a plain, blunt man, that love my country—and that they know *full well* that gave me *public* leave to speak of it! For I have neither *wit,* nor *words,* nor *worth ; action,* nor *utterance,* nor *power of speech,* to stir men's blood—I only speak right on. I tell you that which you *yourselves do know ;* show you my country's wounds, poor, poor *dumb* mouths, and bid *them* speak for me. But, were I *Everett,* and *Everett* I, there were *one* would ruffle up your spirits, and put a *tongue* in every *wound* of my *country,* that should move the *stones* of America to rise and mutiny."

The inaugural ceremonies over, the inaugural oath subscribed before high Heaven and the sovereign people, that he, Abraham Lincoln, would "*preserve, protect, and defend*" the Constitution of the United States, —what followed?

Two long months of time—each hour pregnant with the interests of centuries—wasted and frittered away in a degrading scramble for those places of profit, for which, many had then, and have since, bartered their inestimable birthright.

During the period intervening between the election and the inauguration of Mr. Lincoln, James Buchanan, who, from long experience in the councils of the country, having a perfect understanding of the theory and character of our federative structure of Government; and knowing full well that civil war, once.commenced, would result in consequences too deplorable to be contemplated, endeavored by every means within his power to avert the dreadful catastrophe of armed collision.

And here I desire to record, that while all my political life—as is well known—I openly opposed Mr. Buchanan's presidential aspirations (being favorable to another); opposed him at Baltimore, in the contest with General Cass; went to Cincinnati, and opposed his nomination there ; yes, opposed him in the days of his *power and influence*, when many who now, with base ingratitude, when the sceptre of political power has departed, misrepresent and revile him, crooked the pregnant hinges of the knee, that thrift might follow fawning; now, when the silver crown of accumulated years admonishes him of the hour when the Judge of all the earth shall pronounce whether he kept his oath to " *preserve, protect, and defend*" the Constitution of his country, or broke it on the plea of expediency; now, when hypocrites, and knaves, and thoughtless men, blinded by partisan prejudice, revile, and slander, and would crucify him if they could, I take pleasure in thus publicly repelling these baseless accusations; and, pointing to his message to Congress, of December, 1860, and then pointing to a desolate, broken, and distracted country, declare that history will vindicate the principles asserted in that message, to wit : that the Government of the United States depends for its perpetuity upon the virtue of the people, and the perfect good faith of the separate States, in maintaining, with scrupulous fidelity, *in letter and spirit*, the Federal Constitution ; that war between the States would be disunion, and perhaps centralization and despotism.

During that winter, the Democratic Senators and members struggled hard against the tide of Abolition fanaticism. Various projects of compromise were introduced, and rejected by the Republicans, one of which, that suggested by Senator Bigler, I always regarded as, more than any other, consistent with our Republican form of Government, viz. : To refer the whole question to a vote of the sovereign people. This, like the others, was rejected. Finally, the famous compromise resolutions of the patriot Crittenden—the life-long friend of Henry Clay—were introduced. The Southern members agreed to accept Mr. Crittenden's proposition as a settlement of the difficulty, provided the resolutions were presented or indorsed by the Republican members. They (the Southern members) said, that the excitement and alarm existing in the Southern States, was created by the belief that the Republican party had resolved on an aggressive warfare against their Constitutional guarantees ; and in justification of this apprehension, they pointed to the incontrovertible fact, that a war had been semi-officially inaugurated by sixty-eight Republican Senators and members, endorsing and circulating, under the privilege of their frank, the notorious " Helper Book." They pointed to the John Brown raid into Virginia, at Harper's Ferry, and to the fact that that old cut-throat and horse-thief had been canonized as a hero and martyr, unrebuked by any portion of the Republican party. They pointed to the "personal liberty bills," which disgraced the statutes of every State where the Republican party was dominant. They pointed to the incendiary sentiments uttered by the leaders of that party, both in and out of Congress. All this, and more, they cited, to show that the alarm in the Southern States was not unreasonable, but perfectly natural. Now, said they, you Republican gentlemen can disabuse the minds of our constituents, if they are unreasonably alarmed, by voting for these resolutions of Mr. Crittenden, and this whole difficulty may be amicably adjusted; but if these measures are simply voted for by Democrats, (a two-third vote was necessary to pass the resolutions), the question will not have been changed, but remain precisely as before the vote, and no good will have been effected.

Now, here was the question of *peace* or *war* suspended, as it were, by a thread—the dearest interests of mankind dependent on a ballot. On one side, peace, prosperity, national power, and constitutional liberty—as Washington and our fathers interpreted the name of liberty—on the other side, WAR! CIVIL WAR! with all its accumulating horrors; "States dissevered, discordant, belligerent," demoniac hate, brothers slain by brothers, desolated fields and burning cities, the widow's anguish, the orphan's plaintive wail, the hissing scorn of freedom's votaries in every land, the imprecations coming up from generations of America yet in the womb of time; and, above all, and beyond all, the blasting curse of an offended God, who, when He had taken upon Himself the nature of man, said: "Blessed are the PEACE MAKERS, for they shall be called the children of God." In view of this choice between the good and the evil, between blessings and curses, how did the Republican members of Congress vote on these resolutions of the Kentucky Statesman? *Against them to a man!* And raised the bloody banner of fratricidal war!

Merciful Heaven! was hell unbarred and the demons of perdition permitted at that critical moment to visit our earth, to conjure with devilish incantation those men in the Senate-house clothed with power and responsibility so vast?

How else shall we account for this "most foul and unnatural" conduct? Can we, by applying the ordinary rules of interpretation, account satisfactorily for the rejection by the Republicans in Congress of those peace resolutions? We cannot. It was not in the programme! Other efforts were made by the Democrats. The Peace Congress was convened, and adjourned with the same result. So fearful were the Abolitionists that measures might be adopted in that Convention which would destroy their infernal plot, that letters were written by Senators and members to the Republican Governors of the various States, urging the appointment of men as delegates to the Convention who could be relied upon to oppose all compromise. Here is a specimen of these precious epistles, written by United States Senator Chandler, of Michigan, to the Governor of that State :—

" *To His Excellency, Justin Blair :*

"Governor Bingham and myself telegraphed you on Saturday, at the request of Massachusetts and New York, to send delegates to the Peace or Compromise Congress. They admit that we were right and that they were wrong, that no Republican State should have sent delegates, but they are here and cannot get away. Ohio, Indiana, and Rhode Island are caving in, and there is danger of Illinois, and now they beg us for God's sake to come to their rescue, and save the Republican party from rupture. I hope you will send *stiff-backed* men or none. The whole thing was gotten up against my judgment and advice and will end in thin smoke. Still I hope as a matter of courtesy to some of our erring brethren that you will send the delegates.

" Truly, your friend,

" Z. CHANDLER.

" P. S.—Some of the manufacturing States think that a fight would be awful. Without a little blood-letting this Union will not, in my estimation, be worth a rush.

" WASHINGTON, *February* 11, 1861."

Pennsylvania's most exemplary Executive (?) Andrew G. Curtin, sent to that Peace Congress delegates who he well knew would vote against all compromise. Why did he select David Wilmot as a delegate to that convention? Did he, like Senator Chandler, feel greater solicitude to save the " Republican party" than to save the Union? Did he also think that a little " blood-letting" would be good for the country? I charge upon Governor Curtin, that by sending Judge Wilmot to that convention, he made himself quite as responsible for his share in preventing the adoption of all propositions of compromise and peace which were there persistently voted down, as if he had been present, and had spoken and voted as Judge Wilmot spoke and voted.

It is impossible to crowd into the limits necessary to be observed all the evidence of this most atrocious plot that, like the spectres in King Richard's slumber, pass in rapid review before the mental vision.

Referring again to the period after Mr. Lincoln's inauguration, while the patriots were all engaged in saving as much of the country as would hold the spoils they were industriously apportioning, Commissioners from South Carolina arrived in Washington, and while these men were being hoodwinked by Mr. Seward promising them that the *status* at Fort Sumter should not be disturbed, and the Commissioners, on their part, promising that the gallant Major Anderson and his little band of heroes in Fort Sumter should have every thing in the way of provisions supplied them, until some satisfactory arrangement could, perhaps, be agreed upon, the Administration were engaged in secretly fitting out an expedition in the harbor of New York to provision and garrison the fort, knowing full well that, under the circumstances, these vessels, or the fort itself, would be fired upon. They calculated rightly. An overt act of war was perpetrated; our glorious Star-spangled Banner desecrated, the heart of the Northern masses fired, " the Republican party saved," and the *Union*, it may be, LOST!

The events of that culminating period will form a dark chapter in the history of this bloody drama. It will be recollected that in the latter part of May or first of June, 1861, the telegraph offices in the principal cities were taken possession of by the Government authorities, and among the copies of telegrams seized were those of a certain James E. Harvey, who had been appointed minister to Portugal. These telegrams revealed the fact that Mr. Harvey had been in correspondence with the Rebels at Charleston, South Carolina, and had communicated to them the fact that a fleet of vessels was fitting out in the harbor of New York, designed to provision the garrison at Fort Sumter. This information caused the Rebel authorities to determine to fire upon Fort Sumter, when the said fleet should appear off the Charleston bar. On the 7th of June, the New York *Tribune*, and the Press generally, violently assailed Mr. Harvey for having betrayed the secrets of the Administration in giving this information to the Rebels. When these newspaper articles reached Mr. Harvey at Lisbon, he wrote a "Card," dated Lisbon, July 7, 1861, which was published in the Philadelphia "*North American*," on the 27th of that month, wherein he exonerates himself by declaring that all of the aforesaid correspondence was by authority of the President and Cabinet. In his card he says :

"While holding an official position I am precluded from making declarations which would at once give a satisfactory answer to these slanders." "I do not choose to utter a word at this time, which would in any manner impair the action of the Government, or subject others to harsh and unjust comment, when I know that their motives, like my own, were the purest and best." "The fact is, the Government was in possession of every tittle of the evidence which had accumulated in Washington long before the public seizure was ordered ; several weeks before I left there, and before I had received or accepted any commission. If there was any thing to know it was known fully and entirely, as will be shown whenever necessary. I assert the fact distinctly, without condition or reservation. I submitted to their inspection every line received by telegraph, and never held any other correspondence but that, direct or indirect."

Did Mr. Harvey state the case truly ? *If he did not*, why has he been retained in his important mission from that day till this ?

If he did, what object had the Administration in revealing the fact of this preparation to provision the fort ? Was it that an overt act of rebellion might be committed, "the Northern heart fired," and, in the language of Senator Chandler, in his letter to Governor Blair, "the Republican party saved from rupture ?" or did Mr. Seward believe it to be his duty, as he subsequently avowed, to take care "that the war should be begun by the enemies of the Union ?"

Well, Sumter was fired upon, the Northern heart was fired, and then came the call for seventy-five thousand troops, and then came from the mountains and the valleys, from the rostrum and the anvil, from the merchant's desk and the laborer's ditch, from the gilded saloons of luxury and the rugged cot of penury, from Democrats and Republicans—one grand, spontaneous shout, "The Union ! it must and shall be preserved !"

Then came "Bull Run ;" then the resolutions by Congress, declaring the war to be "for the preservation of the Constitution and the restoration of the Union, with all the rights and dignity of the several States unimpaired," and that when "these objects" should be "attained the war ought to cease," passed unanimously except two votes, one a Northern Abolitionists, the other a Southern Secessionist. In the extremity of alarmcaused by the Bull Run rout, the Republicans voted with the Democrats for these resolutions.

Under the belief that this was the real purpose of the Administration, a vast army of volunteers was obtained, and when the Administration found itself secure behind an impregnable wall of bayonets, the prosecution of the *programme* was resumed.

This narrative having been thus extended, it is out of the question to follow step by step the insidious approaches upon the citadel of liberty, over a violated Constitution, under the hypocritical mask of pretending to defend it. Under the plausible cant, "the Union," "the flag," "the Constitution," and "the unconditional support of the Government," appeals so potent as to reach every patriotic heart; the masses of the people were for a long time deceived, and many still remain under the fatal delusion; notwithstanding that every promise for the restoration of the Union has been broken, and that blessed consummation put more than ever remote by an insane policy, which looks to the sudden emancipation of four millions of negroes, and their elevation to the condition of white men. Feeble man warring in blind fanatical fury, against the immutable laws of God, whose wisdom is made manifest in an inequality in creation "spreading through all life, extending through all extent," observable alike in the vegetable, the mineral, and the animal kingdoms, one seed producing a delicious fruit, another the deadly upas, the beautiful pearl taken from its ocean bed of innumerable and to the superficial mind, worthless, yet in the wise economy of nature, equally valuable pebbles; while in the higher order of creation we have a Milton and the babbling idiot, a Caligula, and a Howard, a Washington, and a Lincoln!

Nearly every vestige of the Constitutional guarantees to the citizen has been ignored, or crushed beneath the heel of tyrannical usurpation.

While the flag of our country is held aloft, as the symbol of the Union of the States, glittering in the splendor of its thirty-four stars, we have it semi-officially announced, by a high functionary of the administration, no less a personage than the Solicitor of the War Department, that the light of ten at least of those stars, is to be extinguished. State lines, says Mr. Whiting, enforcing Charles Sumner's pet scheme, must be obliterated; the domain reduced to a territorial condition; its inhabitants made vassals, with no rights save those which the conqueror chooses to accord to them. VIRGINIA! the Old Dominion! the "mother of States," the State whose very atmosphere is sacred as having first inflated the lungs that gave pulsation to the great heart of Washington; that caught his last expiring breath, and floated his pure spirit up to the eternal throne of heaven; the State, whose "sacred soil",—yes! sacred, indeed, notwithstanding the derision in which the word has been profaned by Abolition traitors, who hate the memory of the *slave-holder* Washington— *above* whose name Wendell Phillips, of Massachusetts, in a public lecture, has placed "on the scroll of fame," the name of *Toussaint Louverture,* the black demon of St. Domingo—whose sacred soil, I say, received

Washington's precious mortal remains! the State of PATRICK HENRY! and where his immortal words were hurled against *British* tyranny—" AS FOR ME, GIVE ME LIBERTY OR GIVE ME DEATH !"—the State of Jefferson, Madison, Monroe, and a host of patriots and martyrs to civil liberty !—the State that gave to the Union—a free and princely gift—all that Northwest Territory, from which have risen some of the grandest commonwealths in the confederacy !—the State, whose influence, statesmanship, and warriors, more than all others, contributed to achieve for us, and bequeathed to us, the priceless blessings of constitutional freedom !—this is the State, to say nothing of all the others, that Mr. Solicitor William Whiting—gorged with the swill of official patronage, puffed as a toad in his own conceit, redolent of perfume from his darling Africans, with the heart of a spider, and the wisdom of a donkey—declares in five solid columns of type, must be reduced to a territorial condition ! Fellow-citizens of America, this is what is called, " *unconditional*" unionism !

The next step was to abolitionize the army, by getting rid, under various pretexts, of as much as possible of the Democratic element among the field officers. Those who were known to be Democrats, incorruptible and true to the legitimate objects of the war, were, from time to time, removed, and their places filled with officers who sympathized with the Abolition projects of emancipation, confiscation, negro troops, and subjugation.

Thus we find that McClellan, the idol of the army, who thrice saved the Capital from capture ; whose brilliant campaign in Western Virginia caused him to be hailed by the public voice as the man for the occasion after the first Bull Run ; whose thorough military science first organized and then disciplined a splendid army, and compelled the enemy to abandon his strong position at Manassas ; who, to splendid engineering qualities, adds a thorough comprehension of the theory of war, understanding perfectly when caution or strategy is desirable, and when dashing impetuosity is necessary, with a temperament peculiarly adapted to either ; whose much-derided pick and spade enabled him to capture the powerful fortifications at Yorktown with scarcely the loss of a battalion, and which said pick and spade have since been adopted by every general who has been successful ; whose rapid movements forced the enemy to make a stand at Williamsburg, there to be beaten and discomfited ; who, after driving the enemy into his capital, approached to within sight of its steeples, and who pledged his military reputation, that, if furnished with McDowell's Corps of forty thousand men, which had been promised him, and which was lying idly at Fredericksburg, he would march into the enemy's capital in less than twelve hours after the word forward should be given ; who repelled the desperate assault on his left wing at Fair Oaks, although, to do so, a lack of sufficient troops required him to endanger his right and centre ; whose brilliant achievement at Hanover Court House kept open the communication with McDowell's Corps in the anxious, though vain hope, that the Administration would give him the troops, in expectation of receiving which his military plans had been adopted ; who, when finally abandoned to his fate in those dismal pestilential swamps of the Chickahominy, his brave army daily reduced by sickness and death, and while the enemy, knowing his weakness and its cause, was gathering up from every quarter an army to crush him—from Corinth where they deliberately walked away from Halleck, and from the Shenandoah Valley where Banks had been driven off by Stonewall Jackson—with military genius, cool brain, and brave heart, and while assaulted by overwhelming odds, swung his army around over thirty miles of territory, with but one road for his trains, and after seven days of continuous and desperate assaults upon his lines, safely encamped his gallant soldiers upon the banks of the James River, thus executing a retreat, which, should he gain a hundred battles, history will record as the grandest and most glorious of his military achievements; who—when General Pope, the pet of the Administration, "whose head-quarters were in the saddle," whose "strategy was to find the enemy," and who knew no such thing in military science as "base lines of retreat," was forced by General Lee to learn that lesson, behind the fortifications which McClellan's pick and spade had prepared for him around Washington—was called with tremulous accents, through pallid and quivering lips to save, as twice before he had saved, the Capital from capture, gathered up with amazing rapidity the scattered, disheartened, and demoralized forces of a routed army, marched against the victorious and exultant foe, drove him from his well selected position at South Mountain, followed him rapidly and again attacked and routed him at Antietam, thus saving Pennsylvania and Maryland from the devastation of invasion and the Capital from capture; then, giving his weary soldiers a brief and absolutely necessary respite for recuperation, and to obtain shoes for their naked feet, crossed the Potomac in pursuit, took possession of the numerous mountain gaps, and while the whole country was excited to exultation in admiration of his triumphant march—suddenly, to the amazement of soldiers and civilians, during the prevalence of a violent snow-storm, received an order at his camp, directing him to report at Trenton, New Jersey!

The blinding snow-drifts that eddied round the tents of that brave Potomac Army, chilled their manly forms, but under the vigilant care of their beloved commander, their hearts were warm. This order from Washington was an ice-bolt driven against every soldier's and civilian's heart, who still fondly clung to the hope of a restored Union under the Constitution of our Fathers, and desired to see the war conducted according to the principles of humanity and civilization.

And so might fame sound her trumpet in eulogizing strains of Buell, and Fitz John Porter, and Naglee, and Andrew Porter, and Burns (not Burnside who distinguished himself only in capturing what was once regarded as an impregnable fortress, to wit, the DOMICILE OF AN AMERICAN CITIZEN, and taking prisoner its garrison in the person of Clement L. Vallandigham), but a braver soldier and a better man, a gentleman as well as a soldier, who knows the value and loves with true devotion the institutions of his country; and a host of others who have been suspended under various shallow pretexts.

The places of these officers have been filled with some honorable excep tions, but wherever it was practicable, with men who have proved subservient tools and parasites at the footstool of power. A majority of the field officers in the higher ranks are of the stripe of Butler, Higginson, Hunter, Shurz, Hooker, whose campaign against McClellan before the War Investigating Committee at Washington, was about as successful as his campaign against Richmond *via* Chancellorsville; and McNeill and Rousseau, who in a public speech in Pennsylvania, in the fall of 1863, spoke of the "Copperheads and traitors who go about cheering for McClellan."

Having got the army firmly in hand by means of this system among the officers, the Administration proceeded gradually to bolder and more shameful invasions of the rights of the people. It would be merely supererogatory to recapitulate. Not a man or woman, and scarcely a child, who is not familiar with these constantly recurring and most atrocious assaults upon the liberty of the citizen. When I use the term *liberty*, I do not mean licentiousness. I speak of undoubted, indefeasible rights, which Webster said belonged to the people as undoubtedly and "as naturally as the right to breathe, and the right to eat."

Mr. Lincoln boldly assumes, in his letter to the Ohio committee, of which Mr. Pendleton was chairman, that, in time of war, he becomes the embodiment of all three of the co-ordinate branches of Government—the law maker, the law interpreter, and the law executor! He goes even a step further, and *makes* laws unknown to our system of jurisprudence—the law of banishment, for instance—and he executes this self-established edict daily, upon all classes of citizens, through his minions sometimes, and occasionally—as in the case of Mr. Vallandingham—by a direct order from himself. Yet Mr. Lincoln has taken a solemn oath to "preserve, protect, and defend" a Constitution whose eighth Amendment reads thus :

"Excessive bail shall not be required, nor excessive fines imposed, nor cruel and unusual punishments inflicted."

The Constitution ordains (in Article 2d of the Amendments) that,

"The right of the people to keep and bear arms, shall not be infringed."

Yet Mr. Lincoln has deprived the people, in whole districts far remote from scenes of hostilities, of this solemnly declared right.

The Constitution declares that,

"In all criminal prosecutions, the accused shall enjoy the right to a speedy and public trial, by an impartial jury of the State and district wherein the crime shall have been committed, which district shall have been previously ascertained by law, and to be informed of the nature and cause of the accusation ; to be confronted with the witnesses against him ; to have compulsory process for obtaining witnesses in his favor, and to have the assistance of counsel for his defence."

Yet Mr. Lincoln has violated every one of these provisions in thousands of instances.

The Constitution declares that,

"No person shall be held to answer for a capital or otherwise infamous crime, unless on a presentment or indictment of a grand jury, except in cases arising in the land or naval forces, or in the *militia*, when in *actual service* in time of war or public danger."

Yet Mr. Lincoln has violated this beneficent provision.

The Constitution declares (Art. 4, Amendments) that,

"The right of the people to be secure in their persons, houses, papers, and effects, against unreasonable searches and seizures, shall not be violated; and no warrants shall issue but upon probable cause, supported by oath or affirmation, and particularly describing the place to be searched and the persons or things to be seized."

Yet Mr. Lincoln has violated, in numerous instances, this wise provision. The Constitution declares, in the third Amendment, that,

"No soldier shall in time of peace be quartered in any house, without the consent of the owner, *nor in time of war*, but in a manner to be prescribed by law."

Yet Mr. Lincoln, through his subordinates, violated this sacred provisions in numerous instances.

The Constitution declares, in the first Amendment, that,

"Congress shall make no law respecting an establishment of religion or prohibiting the free exercise thereof; or abridging the freedom of speech, or of the press ; or the right of the people peaceably to assemble, and to petition the Government for a redress of grievances."

Yet Mr. Lincoln is constantly incarcerating some, and banishing others, whose manhood will not succumb to tyrannical usurpation, preferring death itself to a craven surrender of liberty.

The Constitution provides that, Congress alone shall have power to suspend the writ of *habeas corpus*—that great bulwark against oppression. And this is manifest, from the fact that the allusion to its suspension is found among the negative Congressional provisions. The words are in the fourth clause of the ninth Section of Article 1, and read thus :

"The privilege of the writ of *habeas corpus* shall not be suspended, unless when in cases of rebellion or invasion, the public safety may re-. quire it."

That is, Congress shall *not* have power to suspend it except in designated cases, and for a specific time ; but where is the shadow of authority giving to Congress a right to delegate this stupendous power of a sweeping suspension to a co-ordinate branch of the Government, extending a power, in fact, which it does not itself possess ? Monstrous perversion of the evident meaning of the clause ! Besides, the design evidently was, that the writ might be temporarily suspended only in districts where actual hostilities should exist; where, in fact, judicial authority might become too feeble, because of violent commotion in any particular district, to afford protection to the citizens.

Is there any such commotion in the States of New York, New Jersey, Pennsylvania, or Ohio, as to render it necessary to the public safety, that every citizen of these commonwealths shall be made liable to arrest by a deputy provost-marshal ;—perhaps, by mistake, and, perhaps, from the malice of some informant, who may seek a convenient method of wreaking a petty vengeance;—and the innocent victim hurried off, ignorant even of the nature of the accusation—thrown into a fortress, and his case, it may be, forgotten by the tyrants, through whose infamous despotism he may languish even unto death?

Hence, in his proclamation suspending the writ of *habeas corpus*, Mr. Lincoln has violated another provision of the Constitution.

Section 8, Art. 1, of the Constitution, provides "for organizing and disciplining the militia, and for governing such part of them as may be employed in the service of the United States, *reserving to the States, respectively, the appointment of the officers, and the authority of training* the militia according to the discipline prescribed by Congress."

Now, no legal sophistry, or hair-splitting, can so impose upon common sense, as to induce the belief that Mr. Lincoln has not violated this provision of the Constitution, by sanctioning a conscription which creates a huge consolidated army, in whose ranks, all the States may be represented in each company of each regiment. Thus the New York and Pennsylvania soldier, and the Vermont and Massachusetts, and Ohio and Michigan and Wisconsin men, may be mixed up in every company; destroying that State identity, that State pride, that State sympathy, and, not least, that *State protection*, which the framers of the Constitution designed both for the efficiency of the army, in fostering State emulation, and to guard against that consolidation, which might lead to centralization and usurpation of the legitimate sovereignty of the States.

The Constitution requires (Section 3, Article 2d) that the President shall "take care that the laws be *faithfully executed.*"

May it not be asserted, truthfully, that Mr. Lincoln has "taken care" that the laws shall NOT be faithfully executed?

Witness the arrest and incarceration of that eminent jurist and fearless patriot, the venerable Judge Carmichael, for "faithfully" maintaining the law, under the responsibility imposed by his judicial oath.

The Constitution declares (Section 1, Article 3): That "the judicial power of the United States shall be vested in one Supreme Court, and in such inferior courts as the Congress may from time to time ordain and establish." And (in Section 2, of the same Article): "The judicial power shall extend to *all* cases in law or equity."

Yet Mr. Lincoln has violated this provision by *assuming* judicial powers.

The Constitution (in Section 2, Article 3, 3d clause), declares that "The trial of all crimes, except in cases of impeachment, shall be by jury, and such trial shall be held *in the State,* where the said crimes shall have been committed."

Yet Mr. Lincoln arrests men in one State for alleged crime, and sends them to a fortress in another State, without a trial in either place; and, furthermore, banishes men into "the enemies' country," thereby recognizing the Southern Confederacy, while maintaining that the States composing it are still within the Union, and subject to the laws of Congress, such as emancipation, confiscation, &c., &c.

The Constitution declares (in Section 3, Article 3), that "no person shall be convicted of treason, unless on the testimony of two witnesses to the same overt act, or on confession in open court." Of course, the clause means, that if the conviction shall be by witnesses, *they* shall be *examined* in open court. I have heard the puerile argument advanced, that while the "confession" of an accused must be in "open court," yet if convicted by "witnesses," it may be before a court-martial, or a provost-marshal's board. To such wretched shifts are they driven to palliate their iniquity, torturing and perverting the plainest language ever written.

Mr. Lincoln has clearly violated this important protection to those accused, but guiltless of the high crime of treason.

The Constitution declares (in Section 3, Article 3, second clause), that

"No attainder of treason shall work corruption of blood, or forfeiture, except during the life of the person attainted."

Yet Mr. Lincoln, by signing the Confiscation Bill of the last Congress, has violated this provision, not only in the natural and practical effect of the law, but according to the interpretation now claimed for it, by his warmest political adherents and admirers.

The Constitution declares (Section 3, Article 4), that

"No new State shall be formed or erected within the jurisdiction of any other State."

Yet the State of Virginia has been split in twain, so far as the abolition majority in Congress and Mr. Lincoln has been able to do it.

The Constitution declares (in the second clause of Section 3, Article 4), that

"Nothing in this Constitution shall be *so construed* as to prejudice any claims of the United States, or of *any particular State*."

Has not the partition of Virginia "prejudiced" the claims of that "particular State?" And inasmuch as Mr. Lincoln and his followers pretend that the war is waged to restore the States, including Virginia, to the Union, what becomes of this express and emphatic declaratory clause? In signing that bill, Mr. Lincoln violated this clause of the Constitution.

Article 9 of the Amendments declares,

"The enumeration in the Constitution of certain rights, shall not be *construed* to deny or disparage others retained by the people."

Yet, Mr. Lincoln, either wilfully or ignorantly, has "construed" numerous important provisions according as "military necessity" or expediency, rendered it convenient, and against the interpretation of plain common sense. Witness the attempt to have the electoral vote of several States, controlled by one-tenth of the population.

Article 10 of the Amendments declares that :

"The powers not delegated *to* the United States by the Constitution, nor prohibited *by* it to the States, are *reserved* to the States respectively, or to the people."

Yet, the sovereign rights of the States are violated every day by Mr. Lincoln, under the plea of necessity, expediency, and by gross perversion of the language of the instrument.

The Constitution provides (in Section 2, Article 4, 3d clause,) that,

3

"No person held to service or labor in one State, under the laws thereof, escaping into another, shall, in consequence of any law or regulation therein, be discharged from such service or labor, but shall be delivered up on claim of the party to whom such service or labor may be due."

Now, Mr. Lincoln is bound by his oath to see that this provision is just as faithfully observed in times of commotion and civil war, *so far as it extends to citizens not in rebellion against the United States*, as in time of peace, yet the clause has become obsolete. In fact, the emancipation proclamation virtually wipes it out as with a sponge. Hence, Mr. Lincoln has violated *this* provision.

Finally, the Constitution declares (in the 2d clause of the 6th Article) that,

"This Constitution and the laws which shall be made in pursuance thereof," "shall be the SUPREME law of the land; and the judges in every State *shall* be bound thereby, any thing in the Constitution or laws of any State to the contrary notwithstanding."

And yet Mr. Lincoln has audaciously assumed that HIS WILL shall be the sovereign and supreme law. And judges in the several States who have acted in conformity with their oaths to support this provision of the Constitution, have been, by hirelings and parasites, denounced as traitors to their Government, and even the judicial ermine desecrated in the infliction upon them of personal violence. In permitting this, Mr. Lincoln has violated the sixth Article of the Constitution.

Now, my fellow-countrymen, if any of you will take a copy of the Constitution of the United States and read it carefully, you will find that there is scarcely a fragment of it left. The President and his party in Congress have torn it into ribbons. Will it be said that these innovations are warrantable on account of the civil strife in which we are engaged. How utterly fallacious is this excuse! These are the very times when the sacred provisions of the Constitution should be most jealously guarded; when all should cling to it as "the mariner clings to the last plank, when night and the tempest surround him." What would be thought of the commander of a vessel who, when the hurricane was raging, and his tempest-tossed bark struggling in the trough of the sea, and knowing that he was in the vicinity of dangerous reefs, should throw overboard his chart and his compass?

Time and space admonish me that I must bring this narrative to a close. A folio volume would not contain all the usurpations of this most extraordinary Administration. The servants of the people have assumed to be their masters, and have so conducted themselves during the last three years.

The Hercules of American liberty is now writhing in the toils of the anaconda of despotism. Bravely the young giant struggles for mastery. While the slimy coils twine round his lithe and graceful limbs, millions behold the desperate encounter, and the hearts of freemen throb with alternate hope and fear, as their prayers ascend to Almighty God, that victory may perch on the brow of liberty's champion, and the monster be crushed within his grasp.

Men are as nothing in this great crisis. Whole generations of men pass, in their regular order, into the sepulchre of oblivion. But few individuals live, even in memory, beyond a succeeding generation. Yet, in the progress of time, there are epochs which live for ages; to be referred to by posterity with either blessings or curses. We are passing through one of those periods now! The cause of American liberty is a sacred trust, which each generation of Americans is bound by every principle of honor to transmit unimpaired to its successor. This principle must not be surrendered now. If it should, upon this generation will rest the merited execration of those that are yet in the womb of time.

It is gratifying to reflect that the virtue and good sense of the Democracy have been so signally manifested, in the selection of those in whose persons these great principles are, as we trust, to be vindicated.

Why should I particularly allude to those candidates, my fellow-countrymen? You would not have me pronounce a eulogy upon George B. McClellan! There are some things whose attractions are not enhanced by eulogium: they speak for themselves. To say that the diamond is pure, and clear, and sparkling; that no base material can corrode its fair surface, or cloud its lustre, would not enhance the just admiration entertained for the jewel. Then why write words of commendation of one whose bravery and skill while in service, and whose modest deportment and good taste while in retirement, have commended themselves to every unprejudiced mind? There he stands, clothed in the mail of a spotless reputation, from youth to vigorous manhood—invulnerable! Let the shafts of Abolition malice be hurled with all the force which impotent rage may lend to desperation. Blunted and broken against his impenetrable armor, they fall harmless at his feet; save only those which, glancing, inflict ghastly wounds upon his more vulnerable adversaries.

As much might justly be said of George H. Pendleton: the profound lawyer—the able and fearless statesman—the Christian gentleman. Who dare assail him? Even Malice is dumb, and the tongue of Slander palsied in the effort!

Thanks—most hearty thanks—to the gentlemen of the Convention, who gave us candidates like these at this important crisis.

The responsibility now rests with the people. SEE TO IT THAT EVERY RIGHTFUL VOTE IS DEPOSITED IN THE BALLOT-BOX. Let every man constitute himself a vigilance committee. The loss of a ballot must not be thought of. The jewels that sparkle in kingly diadems will not compare in value with the American freeman's ballot on the eighth of November next.

Do but your duty faithfully, my suffering fellow-countrymen, and when the morning of the ninth of November shall dawn upon our beloved land, the shouts of exultant joy, resounding through beautiful valleys, echoing and re-echoing amidst mountain crags, reverberating through the corridors of the Capitol and within the chambers of the White mansion, shall remind usurpers that the American people are still the SOVEREIGN people, and the only Sovereign that can be permitted to reign on the sacred soil of America.

www.ingramcontent.com/pod-product-compliance
Lightning Source LLC
Chambersburg PA
CBHW021607270326
41931CB00009B/1384